What Are Sound Waves?

Nicola Corsaro

I0808851

ROSEN
COMMON CORE
READERS

Rosen Classroom™

New York

Published in 2014 by The Rosen Publishing Group, Inc.
29 East 21st Street, New York, NY 10010

Book Design: Mickey Harmon

Photo Credits: Cover (boy) Valua Vitaly/Shutterstock.com; cover (background) VikaSuh/Shutterstock.com; p. 5 (trumpet) Sideways Design/Shutterstock.com; p. 5 SergiyN/Shutterstock.com; p. 7 Wesley Aston/Shutterstock.com; p. 9 philippou/Shutterstock.com; p. 11 Alila Sao Mai/Shutterstock.com; p. 13 Africa Studio/Shutterstock.com; p. 15 Mike Brake/Shutterstock.com; p. 17 Dmitry Kalinovsky/Shutterstock.com; p. 19 (vocal cords) hkannn/Shutterstock.com; p. 19 (girl) viki2win/Shutterstock.com; p. 21 (dolphins) Willyam Bradberry/Shutterstock.com; p. 21 (bat) Dr. Morley Read/Shutterstock.com; p. 22 Pavel L Photo and Video/Shutterstock.com.

ISBN: 978-1-4777-2397-5
6-pack ISBN: 978-1-4777-2398-2

Manufactured in the United States of America

CPSIA Compliance Information: Batch #CS13RC: For further information contact Rosen Publishing, New York, New York at 1-800-237-9932.

Contents

Listen Closely

Close your eyes and listen. What do you hear? You probably hear noises coming from all the different things around you. Those noises come to us in the form of sound waves. Do you know what a sound wave is?

A sound wave is a type of energy that we hear. We can't see sound waves, but they're all around us.

Sound waves are what we hear when something makes noise.

Do you know what energy is? It's the ability to do work. Work helps us do things like move, play, eat, and even sleep. There are more kinds of energy than those that move our bodies, though. Energy comes in many forms.

The different forms of energy include heat and light. Sound is one form, too. Energy travels with a sound wave, helping us hear.

Light energy travels faster than sound energy. That's why we see lightning before we hear thunder!

Sound is made when an object vibrates. To vibrate means that something moves back and forth very quickly. The vibrations move tiny pieces of matter in the air, called molecules (MAH-lih-kyoolz). The molecules move and create sound waves.

Have you ever seen something vibrate? Guitar strings vibrate when you pluck them. The top of a drum vibrates when you hit it. That's why both of these instruments make sound.

The six strings on a guitar vibrate differently. That's why all the strings sound different.

How Do We Hear?

Many things happen when sound reaches our ears. First, the waves go into our ears and hit a tiny, thin piece of skin called the eardrum. The waves make our eardrums vibrate. The vibrations move the tiny bones in our ears, which carry sound to the **brain**.

The brain can tell the difference between all kinds of sounds. That's how we hear people talking, feet tapping, music, and other noises.

Our ears work hard to help us hear.
Take a look at what happens inside your ears!

Inside the Ear

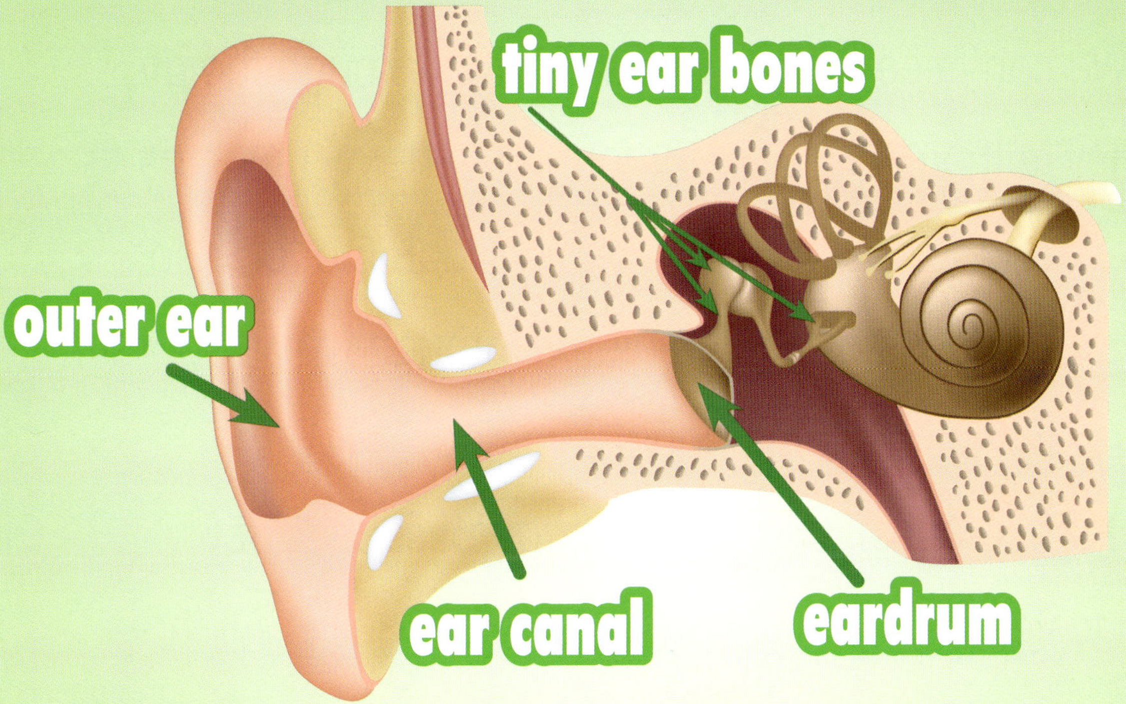

Step 1: The outer ear collects sounds.

Step 2: Sound travels through the ear canal.

Step 3: Sound hits the eardrum and makes it vibrate.

Step 4: The eardrum makes three tiny bones vibrate.

Step 5: The vibrations pass through the eardrum and go to the brain.

Step 6: The brain tells us what the sound is.

We can't see sound waves moving through the air, but they're there. Unlike other forms of energy (such as light), sound waves need to travel through matter, also known as a medium. The mediums through which sound can travel include solids, liquids, and gases.

Sound waves travel fastest through solids. They travel faster through liquids than through gases. All three mediums help sound waves reach our ears.

Children, men, and women use their ears to help them hear sound waves.

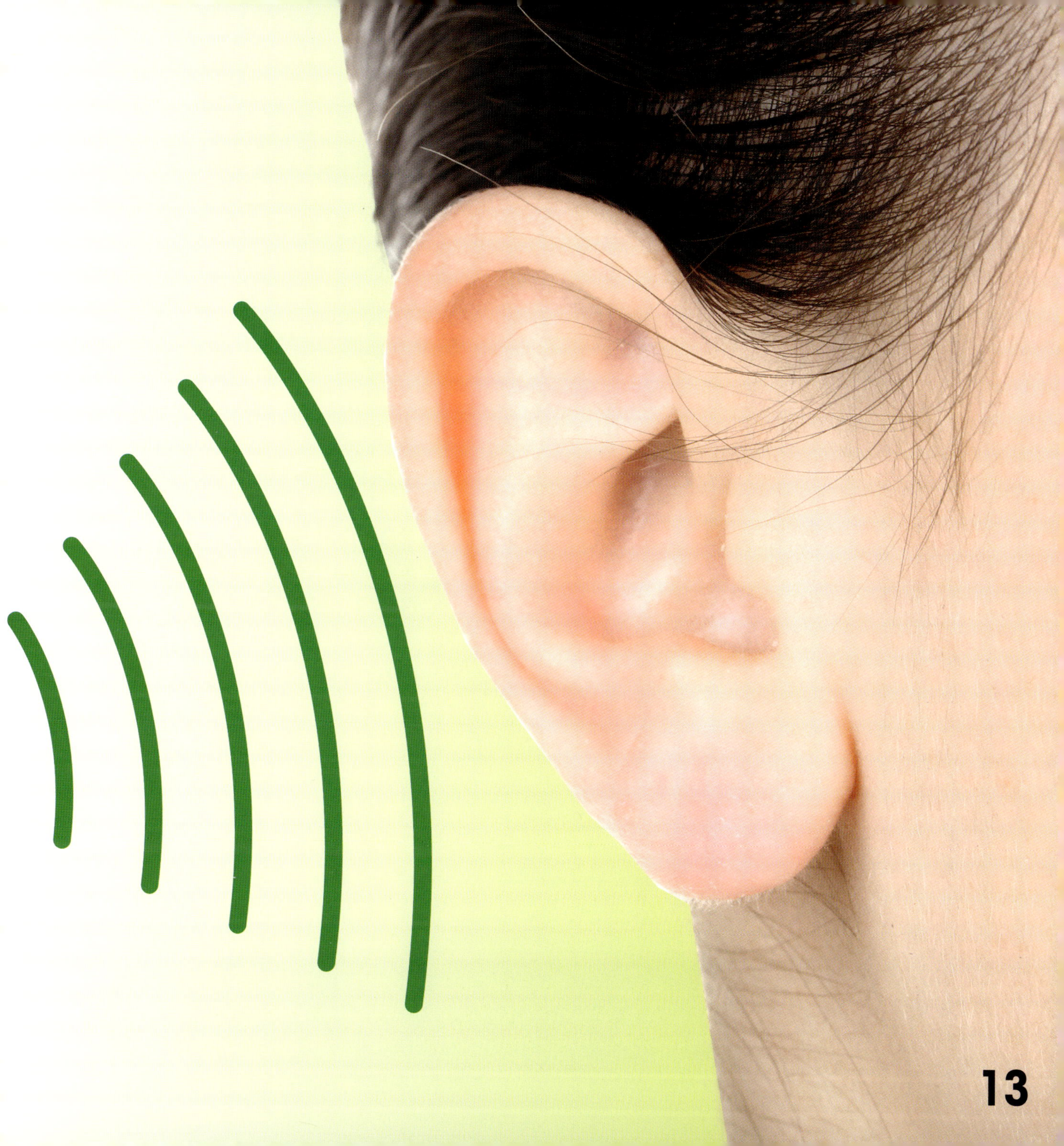

Loud or Soft?

One way we measure sound is with volume. Volume tells us how loud or soft a sound is. The amount of energy in a sound wave gives the sound its volume.

Loud sounds have a lot of energy. You can hear loud sounds without being near the **source** of the sound. The energy helps the sound reach our ears from far away. Soft sounds only have a little energy. You have to be close to the source in order to hear them.

A fire truck's siren is very loud. Can you imagine how loud it must sound to men and women in the truck?

ENGINE

We hear a lot of noises every day. We have to be careful, though, because hearing too many loud sounds can hurt our ears. Luckily, sounds can be blocked and **absorbed**.

Sound waves are blocked when they can't travel through certain objects. Closing a door or window makes noises sound quieter. That's because the doors and windows keep some of the sound waves from reaching us.

People who work around a lot of noise may wear earplugs to protect their hearing. The earplugs keep most of the sound from reaching their ears.

High and Low

We also measure sound with pitch. Pitch tells us how high or low a sound is. It's caused by how fast or slow something vibrates. Fast vibrations make high pitches. Slow vibrations make low pitches.

Your voice has pitch because your **vocal cords** vibrate to produce sound. Children's voices are usually high-pitched. Adults, especially men, usually have low-pitched voices.

Pitch and volume are different. Just because something vibrates slowly doesn't mean it's softer. Low sounds can be very loud!

vocal cords

I Hear an Echo

One of the coolest things about sound is that it can make echoes. Have you ever heard an echo? It happens when sounds bounce off objects and return to where they came from.

Some animals, such as bats, use echoes to help them move and find food. When a bat's chirp bounces off food or an object, the echo tells the bat where the object is. Then they can find it or move around it.

Many animals use echoes, such as dolphins, bats, and birds!

Sound Is Everywhere

Sound is all around us. Think about how sound is important in your life. What would it be like if you couldn't hear or make noises?

Paying attention to different sounds is a great way to understand the world around us. Without it, our lives would be very different!

Glossary

absorb (uhb-ZOHRB) To take in.

brain (BRAYN) The organ in the head that controls your body.

source (SORS) The place where something begins.

vocal cords (VOH-kuhl KOHRDZ) Tissues in the throat that vibrate and make noise when air passes over them, allowing us to speak.

Index